How to Clean Your Home Organically

De-Stress Your Surroundings

Kay Newton

Praise For *How To Clean Your Home Organically*

"I very much enjoyed this book, which is so odd. Who likes cleaning? Not I!

I appreciate the tone, the back story and the simplicity of the system. And I especially appreciate the education in the second half concerning nasty ingredients found on the shelves at the local stores, the list of natural substitutes and how to use them. Last, but not least, those hacks!

Thank you for putting this short book together. Easy to read, easy to comprehend, easy to implement."

Andrea Schmitz, USA

"What a great little book to have when you need that extra boost to clean.
For me cleaning can be quite a chore, so this systematic way makes it quite fun to do!
I love the organic cleaning products and tips, especially as bicarbonate of soda, vineagar and lemon juice are my favourite cleaning products.
Thank you Kay for writing so clearly and simply."

Linda Ledwidge, Spain

"This book is an eye-opener! I made the mistake of putting off putting my feet up to read this until I'd finished my big spring clean - silly mistake and I won't do that again!

This book is brilliant. The list of natural alternatives to the harsh and often dangerous chemicals we use all the time was incredible. I knew lemons were useful, but I'd no idea just how useful. Oh for a lemon grove in the garden! As ever, your writing is enlightening and educational, without ever being patronising. You write with such warmth and passion, it's infectious! This book is staying with me wherever I am - along with the bottle of vodka in my cleaning box - for mirrors, of course!"

Andrea Steel, UK

"This book has made me really think about the way I want to run my Estate Management business. I am not sure my cleaning ladies are going to be behind me in changing to all-natural cleaning products, yet it makes total sense! I have the feeling my profits at the end of the year will be happier too."

Eva Marie Burns, EM Properties and Services, Spain

With Thanks

I am grateful to Ian and Vanessa from Greenwave Promotions, who have been on an editing journey with me for the past few years! I am grateful for their continued guidance, nudging me further down the road to greatness.

A big thank you to Marie Tillbert for the book cover design.

To all my peeps who keep me motivated and get me out of bed in the morning with positive words of encouragement and inspirational stories.

And finally to the four men in my life. I love them very much; James, Max, Tom and Steven.

About

Kay is an award-winning international speaker, enthusiastic author, blogger, artist and Midlife Stress Buster. Her clients love her straight talking and practical stress-relieving holistic help and support.
Kay's books include:

The Art of Midlife Stress Busting – Seven Steps to Declutter Your Mind Without Pills or Potions

Tips And Tricks For Stress-Free Downsizing - A Step by Step Guide to Moving On

She co-authored the ebooks in the *Quick Fix For* series, and is a contributing author to *Hot Women Rock* and *A Journey of Riches*.

Kay hails from Leeds in Yorkshire, England. In her early 20s she jumped on board a 'gin palace' leaving Hull for sunnier shores in Spain, and refused to swim back. She set up her own business looking after holiday homes for the rich and famous, became an eco-landlady extraodinaire, and the mother of two boys. She has been married for over 25 years.

In 2015, after a 30-year dream life on the Spanish island of Mallorca, Kay and her husband decided that rather than having an empty nest, they preferred 'no nest'. Leaving their two grown boys to fend for themselves, they decluttered and downsized to a two-roomed house with a tin roof next to a pristine beach on the island of Zanzibar, off the coast of Tanzania. Kay now lives a life free of unnecessary stress, and has never been happier.

Beachcombing one day, she decided it's time to focus on ridding the Boomer generation of unnecessary stress. She founded the Midlife Virtual Retreat, a weekly online session to relax, rejuvenate and have fun. You can join her here: https://www.facebook.com/TheMidlifeStressBuster/

You can also find Kay Newton The Midlife Stress Buster here:
https://www.kay-newton.com/

Table of Contents

Foreword

This book is based on thirty years' experience running a house management/guardiennage business in Mallorca, Spain, and a decade spent as a personal development coach, caring confidante and Midlife Stress Buster.

Today, stress is considered a leading cause of death in people over 50. Midlifers have a lot to deal with: ageing parents, empty nests, boomerang kids, worries over pension shortfalls, mortgages or health care plans, caregiving, the loss of a loved one, ill health, divorce, moving home, loneliness, isolation - the list seems endless.

In the US alone, 1 in 10 people over the age of 45 are thought to suffer from stress-related anxiety and depression. Worries about money, work, politics, the economy, relationships, health, and personal and national security are cited as causes (https://www.apa.org/news/press/releases/stress/2011/final-2011.pdf).

Many at midlife feel stressed, trapped in a downward spiral they can't escape. It's said that women suffer from stress more than men. The constant need to consume and hoard, and a tendency to live amongst clutter also contribute to stress. A sedentary lifestyle and unhealthy eating habits add their two-penn'orth to a general feeling of dissatisfaction with our lives.

The medical profession treats stress and anxiety by prescribing anti-depressants, which in turn cause other health issues. The good news is: with a little work midlifers can glide gracefully into old age, feeling calmer and more content, while embracing the concept of being *Sensibly Selfish*.

Sensibly Selfish is all about giving yourself permission to be the first priority, for the highest good. When you put yourself first, you can focus on your own well-being, and thus be in the right place energetically to be able to help others. Just like in the aircraft emergency protocol, you have to put on your own oxygen mask before you can help others.

One of the factors which contributes to stress is overwhelming mess, either mental or physical. When you clear your home of dirt, you also clear your thoughts.

This book will cover:
Kay's unique hacks for cleaning a home, and the organic products she uses, so that you can clean your home quickly, efficiently and safely, without missing a single corner or wasting time having to backtrack over areas missed. The simple steps outlined are based on common sense, and are easy to follow. In the resources section, you will find links to other articles, recipes and equipment.

This book is not for you right now if you:
• Dislike following simple step-by-step procedures
• Have no interest whatsoever in cleaning
• Are in the process of decluttering or downsizing your home
• Need to spring clean your mind first

For help with these matters, please visit the resource section at the end of this book, where you can find other titles by Kay.

Introduction

I have always loved the idea of living in a round house, I'm not sure why. Perhaps it's the thought that living in a round dwelling means there will be no corners where dust can collect! Years ago I tried to persuade my husband that living in a Mongolian yurt would be awesome. I'm still working on it. Here in Africa I get quite jealous when I see the local ladies, broom in hand, sweep their small round homes gracefully and with huge smiles; it seems to take them less than no time.

Unless you are one of those fortunate people who live in a round home, I'm acutely aware that cleaning takes time, especially in the corners! Until recently I was the only person in my home who was thorough about cleaning! If I left the housework to my husband or our two boys, they conveniently became blind to the corners.

Living in a dirty, messy house is stressful. It's difficult to find things, there is a higher risk of allergies, asthma, infestation and stomach-related illness. Reducing the risks by cleaning creates more space for the positive things in life. It's worth bearing in mind that we all have different standards of cleanliness. Some people prefer to ignore the dirt around them, others like to clean occasionally. Some have an obsessive cleaning disorder. Thank goodness we're all so different, or the world would be a very boring place!

In our little house in Zanzibar I have a cleaner twice a week, and although I love the luxury, I still cannot get the old habits out of my system. When I see untidiness or dirt I have to deal with it. By devoting a few minutes each morning to tidying our home, I can focus on the task at hand as I work on my computer. I find my mind clears enabling me to use my listening skills to the maximum and become the best Stress Buster I can possibly be. It's my passion in life, and it makes me excited about getting up each day. Cleaning the home makes for a clean working environment, which makes sense since I work from home!

I also love the fact that I have a minimalist lifestyle. In order to live the life we do I have had to ditch huge amounts of mental and physical baggage. Ditching baggage is the best way to clear space for things that you want in your life. I love the essentialism of my life here in Zanzibar, knowing that when I leave, it will be with just a 20kg suitcase containing the only possessions that matter to me - and even that feels far too much! It's not what this book about, though it's true that having fewer possessions certainly makes cleaning easier.

Keeping dust at bay can be lonely work. It's also a thankless and never-ending job. Living in the dusty countryside doesn't help! Yet I love a clean home, it gives me space to write. When the house is untidy, my thoughts also seem to be untidy. The problem is, when you are the only one who cleans, and you can't function unless your home is clean, the last thing you need is for it to take up so much of your time. Otherwise, you would never do anything else but cleaning!

My first experience of cleaning as a professional was when I worked in the private yacht industry, where cotton buds for cleaning the minutiae around the toilet bowl were compulsory items in the cleaning basket. We won't go to that extreme in this book! Yet once you have been trained to spot dirt, it becomes very difficult not to notice.

I took my cleaning expertise into my very first business in Mallorca, where I took care of holiday homes for the rich and famous. With ample money and a lifestyle which included servants, the elite demanded and expected a high standard from our cleaning services. The cleaning we offered had to be quick and efficient. At one point I had over 30 members of staff. There was always something to clean!

As a team, we tried many different ways to become even quicker and more efficient. If it didn't work we went back to the drawing board and tried a different technique. We didn't invent the wheel: if a method worked for others, that's where we started. For example, our grandmothers had used newspaper and vinegar to clean windows, so we also gave it a go. The trouble was, we found that the ink in modern newspapers ended up on our hands and uniforms, as well as the windows! When a new style of mop came out we would give it a trial run and then decide if we wanted to carry on using it. We happily adopted anything that shaved another 5 minutes off our workload.

Through the years we found that working in teams inspired energy and motivation, making it the best way of all. We created a simple system to ensure that all surfaces were cleaned thoroughly, nothing was forgotten, and we all knew what was expected of us. It took a while before we had a system that worked, irrespective of who was cleaning or where we were working. The system we developed is the one described in this book.

Over the years I have realised that having a clean house does not mean you need to drench it in chemicals. My past life as a professional cleaner using powerful, toxic cleaning agents has affected my body. When I'm close to supermarket household products, I notice my beathing changes rapidly. My skin is sensitive to the slightest contact with those man-made concoctions, and I have begun to develop allergies to certain products. There is a better way of cleaning, without using artificial chemicals, and I describe the reasons why you need to do this and how you can clean using simple natural organic alternatives in the second section of this book.

As a 'heart-based entrepreneur' I love to share my knowledge so that you can also do things the easy way. By following the principles outlined here, you will save a lot of time and stress, and have a perfectly clean home. Which means you can move on to having some *Sensibly Selfish* time for yourself, even if it's just a 'Mini Me' moment. You can use the information below either for cleaning you home on a daily basis, or for a thorough annual spring clean. The principle is the same.
Here's how it works...

How To Clean

"Cleaning is something you do that nobody notices until you don't do it" - Unknown

Before you begin cleaning you need to consider what you are going to clean, how you are going to do it, and what materials you will need. I break the task down into bite-sized chunks. I always clean in the same way, beginning at the entrance door of the room. I prepare cleaning materials in advance, and place them together so they are always handy. I hate wasting time through having to break off and find a new duster or make a new batch of homemade pesticide.

Think - A Series of Boxes
To begin the cleaning process all you have to do is imagine the house as a series of boxes. Boxes have 6 sides. A top, bottom and four walls. The first box is the actual house, then you can break each room into boxes too. Living in a round house, the principle still applies, you just have fewer sides!

The Ceiling
The ceiling is always the first thing to clean and the floor is always the last.
Enter any room and clean left to right from the door entrance, with no exceptions. This means that if you have to break off, you know where you have reached.

Check the ceiling for cobwebs and dust etc, working around from the entrance of the room until you return to where you started.

The Walls
Everything on the four walls is cleaned methodically, left to right, top to bottom. Don't miss anything out, especially behind pictures and paintings! Always think internally to externally.

When spring cleaning a wardrobe, for example, clean the outside top first. Next, remove all the contents, and clean the wardrobe. (This may be a good time to lift it and clean underneath if it's not a built-in wardrobe). Clean and replace the contents, then tackle the rest of the outside.

Please note that I did not say spend time decluttering the contents of your wardrobe. Decluttering is an entirely different subject to cleaning, although they're related. It's often better to tackle decluttering first, as a separate activity. If you would like to know more about decluttering there is a link in the resources section to the ebook I co-authored with Pat Duckworth *The Quick Fix for Decluttering*.

Centre of the Room
When you have cleaned all four walls and any furnishings in the room, move to the centre of the room. Repeat the procedure described above.

Floors
Vacuum or sweep, then mop the floors, always working towards the entrance of the room so you don't have to stand on the clean, wet sections. I really hate to see a soaking wet floor. Sloshing water around does not clean the floor well. In fact, when it has dried it can look streaky and dirtier than before you started. If the floor has been vacuumed or brushed beforehand then a well-wrung mop will do a better job.

Special Areas - Kitchen and Bathrooms
The most difficult rooms to clean are always the kitchen and bathrooms. It's easy to underestimate how long these areas will take, especially when spring cleaning. As a rule of thumb, I always double the time I first estimated.

The same cleaning principle applies as described above. Clean the ceilings first. Then clean internal cupboards from the entrance of the room, working from left to right. When you have cleaned all the cupboards, tackle surfaces along the walls, until you reach the centre of the room. Finish with the floor.

For information about cleaning specific items such as ovens, taps, mirrors and so on, see my *Top Ten Hacks For Specific Areas* below.

Notes
- Change cleaning equipment according to the order of the surface to be cleaned next, for example, windows, frames, ceramics, and so on. Don't do all the windows then all the frames - it's too easy to forget a section of the room.
- I carry my equipment around in a basket, so everything is to hand and can be returned to the basket after use.
- If you are spring cleaning soft furnishings like curtains and cushion covers, remove all the fabrics in the same way: enter the room, start on the left of the door and take down all fabrics until you are back at the entrance of the room again. Then do the same for the middle of the room.
- Remember, it's important to clean as you go along, including the windows!
- If you're spring cleaning and using the to-do list you created while decluttering, you may want to paint the walls or do specific DIY jobs. To do so, shift all moveable furniture into the centre of the room and cover with dust sheets. Clean furniture items well before returning them to their rightful positions.
- Do external cleaning of the home after completing all the cleaning jobs on the rooms and hallways.

Team Work
Work always goes faster when you are part of a team, so why not invite friends over to give you a hand? Later you can reciprocate and help them in their home. When you clean as a team, the workload is a little different, and so is the system. So that you don't get in each other's way, one person begins in the kitchen and another in the bathroom.

Once these are clean (apart from the floors) the remaining rooms can be dealt with, each person taking care of a room on their own.

For example, if you have a two-story house, after cleaning the kitchen and bathrooms, which always take the longest, you both begin on the bedrooms before tackling the downstairs rooms. Always work so that clean surfaces are behind you as you progress towards the exit.

Tip: If you have bed linen to change, two of you can do double beds more efficiently.

The first person to finish their tasks begins vacuuming or sweeping all the floors, starting from the furthest point away from the main door. The other person follows with the mop, washing the floors, always working towards the main entrance of the house. The aim is for both to finish at about the same time.

Ten Quick Cleaning Hacks

- If your home feels untidy and you don't have time to clean it all, set a timer for ten minutes and pretend your mother-in-law just phoned to say she will be arriving in 15 minutes! Get your cleaning box out and see what a difference you can make in spurts of energy.
- Clean in sections. Do a room a day over a week, rather than having to allocate a whole day to cleaning.
- There is nothing worse than having to sort and tidy before cleaning. Take the hard work out of the cleaning by having the rooms ready to clean. Remove the laundry, fold away clothes, put away toys and other clutter BEFORE you even begin to clean.
- Make it an exercise routine. Add your favourite music and get a workout as well as a clean home.
- Wear a set of old 'cleaning' clothes. You'll only do half a job if you worry about getting dirty!
- Be prepared: have your cleaning products in one place, ready in a basket or box so all you have to do is pick them up.
- Remember: if your cleaning products don't fit into one basket you have too many - simplify! Have a look at the next section for the things I have in my basket.
- Don't forget to include the rubbish bag! You're bound to find things that need throwing out, as well as the dirt that you need to put in the bin. Have a bag ready so you don't need to break off cleaning to find one.
- Make every movement count: no backtracking, just follow the steps above. As well as turning it into an exercise routine, remember to use both hands. You can spray with the left and wipe with the right!
- Make a note in your diary, how long it took or where you got to, especially if you're spring cleaning or cleaning in bursts. Then you will know how much time to allocate for the next clean.

Cleaning Materials

"Someone sent me an email about using vodka for cleaning around the house. It worked! The more vodka I drank the cleaner the house looked!" - Unknown

We all have our favourite cleaning products. As the market develops and offers different ones it can be difficult to decide what to buy. When I first cleaned homes I used to buy only the 'best' products on the market for each particular job. I failed to read the contents properly. Over the years this has resulted in my body becoming highly sensitive to chemicals and man-made perfumes.

Over the past decade the media has helped us become aware of toxic chemicals in our food, yet many of us ignore the chemicals under our sink or in our cosmetics. We are exposed to toxic chemicals in our home on a daily basis. For example, an average UK household may contain 62 different poisons at any one time.

Manufacturers usually print warnings on the label about possible reactions to their products, such as headaches from noxious fumes and skin irritation from splashes. If challenged they argue that their products only contain a relatively small amount of toxic ingredients, and are therefore safe. Few studies look into the dangers of using products in combination, and the results of daily, weekly, monthly and lifetime exposure to them.

Some chemicals build up in the body over time, causing toxic stress and polluting the body. This may lead to chronic problems later in life. Exposure to household products has been linked with asthma, weight gain, reproductive disorders, cancer, hormone disruption and other conditions.

The products I now have in my cleaning basket are some of the classic ones used throughout history, and they are all natural. I will share the list with you shortly. First, it's important to remember that many common cleanin products available from supermarkets include parabens and other harmful chemicals.

Parabens are added to products to prolong their shelf life. They are thought to cause hormonal issues in humans. With the sharp increase in cancer and chemical-related diseases today, you may want to do more research into the products on your shelf.

Look out for these words on product labels the next time you go shopping:

1. TRICLOSAN
You will find Triclosan in dishwashing detergents and antibacterial products. Because it is an aggressive antibacterial agent it can promote the growth of antibiotic-resistant bacteria. It is also thought to disrupt hormone function.

2. QUATS (Quarternary Ammonium Compounds)
Found in fabric softener, either in liquid form or sheets, and in antibacterial products. Like Triclosan, QUATS promote antibiotic-resistant bacteria. QUATS also irritate the skin and may cause severe asthma.

3. BUTOXYETHANOL
With an unpronounceable name like this, it's bound to be poison! Glycol ethers are the key ingredient of window cleaners, yet US law does not require them to be disclosed on the product label. Glycol ethers are known to cause sore throats when inhaled. At high levels glycol ethers can also contribute to narcosis, pulmonary oedema, and severe liver and kidney damage. These products should only be used if the room is well ventilated, and preferably never used at all!

4. AMMONIA
You can still buy neat ammonia off the shelves in Spain. You will also find it hidden in many polishing agents, especially for bathrooms, sinks and windows. It evaporates quickly, immediately affecting the user who inhales it.

Ammonia can cause or exacerbate chronic bronchitis and asthma.

Warning: ammonia should never be mixed with bleach, because the reaction between the two produces a highly toxic gas.

5. CHLORINE
Chlorine is found in scouring powders, mildew removers, laundry whiteners and toilet cleaners. It is also in domestic drinking water, so exposure to chlorine is chronic. It enters the body through the skin, by inhalation and by drinking. Research shows that chlorine causes severe respiratory issues and thyroid disruption.

6. PHTHALATES
Phthalates are a group of chemicals used to soften and increase the flexibility of plastic and vinyl. They are found in plastic bottles, cosmetics and personal care products, perfume, hair spray, soap, shampoo, nail polish, skin moisturisers, flexible plastic and vinyl toys, shower curtains, wallpaper, vinyl miniblinds, food packaging, plastic wrap, wood finishes, detergents, adhesives, plastic plumbing pipes, lubricants, medical tubing and fluid bags, solvents, insecticides, medical devices, building materials and vinyl flooring. Phthalate is listed as "reasonably anticipated to be a human carcinogen". Men are known to have a significantly lower sperm count when phthalates are found in their bloodstream.

7. SYNTHETIC MUSK
(Fragrance, musk ketone, musk xylene, galaxolide tonalide)
These are my worst nightmare: I really suffer from the fragrance industry. My main gripes are having to dash through duty-free at airport, or even worse, sitting next to someone who has just tried countless perfumes at duty free before getting on the plane! And I can't go inside high street shops due to the perfume they diffuse.

Most 'smelly' stuff on the high street - including the most expensive perfumes - have no natural aroma: the smells are man-made. Air fresheners, dish soaps, even the clothes you buy, if it has a smell, it's likely to be one of the above chemical fragrances. The most common types of musks used in consumer products are nitro-musks (e.g. musk ketone and musk xylene) and polycyclic musks (e.g. galaxolide and tonalide).

These chemicals are known to be endocrine disruptors. Exposure occurs mainly through inhalation or contact with the skin. If absorbed by the skin, they go straight to the internal organs. A further concern is that we are now exposed to higher levels of these chemicals through the ingestion of foods such as fish, which have absorbed them.

8. SODIUM HYDROXIDE
Sodium hydroxide is found in oven cleaners and drain clearers. It is extremely corrosive. It can cause severe burns in contact with the skin or eyes. It can cause respiratory issues if inhaled.

9. PERCHLOROETHYLENE OR PERC
PERC is a neurotoxin. It can be found in dry-cleaning solutions, spot removers, and carpet and upholstery cleaners. The immediate effects of inhalation include dizziness and loss of coordination. It is also considered to be a carcinogen.

My Top Fifteen Favourite Natural Cleaning Products

Ten years ago I decided to go as ecological as I could with my cleaning products, and turned to the eco-brands on the supermarket shelves. Now, in Zanzibar I have gone a step further: I use only natural ingredients and make my own products. A few glass jars later, my cleaning box is totally organic and I feel a lot healthier.

Now you know what chemicals to avoid in your cleaning products, you may also like to know more about some of the hidden chemicals in your toiletries and make-up. I have created a FREE gift for you with information about this. You can find out how to download it at the end of this book. My second FREE gift will give you the organic homemade alternatives too.

Below are the natural and organic items I love to use for cleaning my home. Look down the list and you will probably find a lot of the ingredients in your kitchen cupboard, which of course makes complete sense: if you can eat it safely, it should be healthy, good for the environment and non-toxic. Treat yourself to a big wicker basket or a wooden box with a handle, a few small glass jars for your concoctions, some cleaning cloths, and you are ready to clean. You won't need hundreds of products. If it doesn't fit into one box or basket, then it's time to simplify. Having too many creates stress, and cleaning shouldn't be stressful.

Take a look at the list below. You will know some ingredients already, while others may be new to you. I recommend starting with a few items. Get to know their cleaning potential, and add more as you go along.

1. LEMON or LIME JUICE
I use this to remove stains from wooden kitchen work surfaces. Squeeze a quantity of juice, spread it liberally on the surface and leave it overnight. The next day, scrub off the excess and apply a coat of olive oil to seal the wood.

also makes the work surface hygenically safe for rolling dough or pastry.

Lemon juice acts as a natural, non-toxic alternative to bleach, so you can use it wherever vinegar is mentioned throughout this book. When I lived in Spain, I had a citrus grove of 48 trees, so I was never short of lemons for cleaning.

It's also a fabulous stain remover, insect deterrent and odour-buster (just place half a lemon in your fridge). Mixed with salt it makes a good pan scrubber, too.

2. BAKING SODA PASTE
Baking soda is my go-to cleaner, along with vinegar. If it needs cleaning, begin here!

It may take a little more time to clean even the grimiest of ovens. On the plus side, you don't have to wear a gas mask as you clean. Just mix half a cup of baking soda with three tablespoons of water and you're ready to go.

Mixing vinegar and baking soda together also makes a good dishwasher and washing machine cleaner. It will also unblock drains.

3. BEESWAX
There is nothing like the smell of this natural product when applied to wooden furniture, it really makes the woodwork glow! You can buy beeswax at many outlets, or you can make your own by melting one cup of beeswax in three cups of olive oil and adding an essential oil of your choice.

4. BICARBONATE OF SODA
An all-round general cleaner that can even replace your washing powder. This is a product all homes should have in abundant supply. I use it to remove stains in the bathroom and kitchen, as well as fingerprints on the wall.

5. BIOKLEEN

This company has a huge range of eco-products for those of us who really can't be bothered to make our own. The chlorine-free oxygen bleach powder made for sinks and baths is a fabulous product, great for stubborn stains.

Note: I am sure that as time goes by I will review this list, add new items and take off others, though the basic philosophy will remain the same. If it's a natural product and doesn't harm the environment, then it can stay.

6. BON AMI POWDER

If you don't want to make your own cleaning products, you may want to check out Bon Ami. The company was formed before the chemical revolution and still makes products from natural ingredients, such as ground feldspar and baking soda. Think vegan cleaning products! The link to their website is in the resource section. I love their simplicity and have a bottle hidden in my cleaning box so no-one else can use it.

7. BORAX POWDER

Borax is a natural chemical also known as sodium tetraborate decahydrate. Not only is it great for cleaning and washing clothes, it also makes a fabulous insect killer moth- repellant, disinfectant, fungicide and herbicide. It is not widely available today due to legislation (it can be harmful if ingested, or if it gets in your eyes). You can buy it under its chemical name on eBay. Look out for the pure form or '20 Team Mule'. Please read the informative blog from Wellness Mama in the resources section at the end of this book for lots of information on borax. Also, do you own due diligence to decide whether you wish to use borax

8. CASTILE SOAP

Originally made in Spain from olive oil and ash, Castile soap is once again gaining popularity. It has a pH value of about 8.9. This is around the same level as baking soda slightly more alkaline than mild dish soap, yet less alkaline than bleach or corrosive tile cleaners.

When added to water, its grease-grabbing qualities make it great for cleaning counters, sinks, bathtubs, floors, or toilets. It can also get rid of insects that infest houseplants, and can even replace laundry detergent. Because Castile soap is biodegradable and non-toxic, it's safe to use on pets and around kids. You can even clean vegetables with it, as long as it's sufficiently diluted.

Castile soap should not be used with vinegar, because they work against each other and you will end up with white stains everywhere.

9. ESSENTIAL OILS
If you must have the smell of perfume in your cleaning prodcuts, you can turn to natural essential oils for great aromas. Adding tea tree oil to your vinegar, for example, will not only make everything smell fresh, it also has natural antibacterial and antifungal properties. I turn to the fragrance of lavender, ylang-ylang and vanilla essential oils on a regular basis. There are so many to choose from, I'm bound to have a new favourite next week!

Take care when using essential oils. Always consult a qualified aromatherapist for guidance, and don't allow the undiluted oil to come in contact with your skin. They should only be ingested under professional guidance. For more information on my use of essential oils to Bust Stress see the link to my post in the resources section below.

10. HOMEMADE PESTICIDE
This is great for both indoor and outdoor plants. Get an empty bottle with a spray attachment, fill it with water, add two cloves of garlic, tobacco leaves or any old cigarette stubs you can find and a few drops of washing up liquid. Leave in a sunny spot for one week or more, until it reeks! Then spray on the plants. Top up the bottle as necessary.

11. MICROFIBRES
I'm a great fan of microfibre cleaning cloths, even though they are synthetic (*see my cautionary note below). They clean efficiently and quickly, so they're great time savers.

Just add a few drops of water to a cloth, then use a dry cloth to buff. Bathroom sinks, mirrors and taps are gleaming in no time. You don't need potions or poisons, just water.

The mop system I have means I no longer use an electric vacuum cleaner. First, I attach the microfibre dusting cloth, which attracts dirt like a magnet attracts pins, then I switch to the mop and wash the floor. I don't have carpets, although I use the mop to sweep over rugs; it collects all the dog hairs I can see.

Not only do the microfibre cloths save time, expense and water, they also need no chemicals, plastic bottles or electricity. (See Resources.)

*When buying microfibre products I take care to choose a supplier whose products are guaranteed to last. Then I make sure I wash the cloths out by hand, NOT in the washing machine. There's a growing concern that microfibres released into the ocean via washing machines are harming fish populations. I may need to change my use of microfibres in the future, as research produces further information about their environmental impact.

12. OLIVE OIL
Place a few drops on a soft cloth or kitchen towel and apply to stainless steel. It makes it look shiny without the streaks, so simple and quick.

13. SAGE
The ancient practice of Smudging is thought to naturally clear the air of negative energies and harmful bacteria. It also leaves the room smelling fresh and clean. It is fabulous way to finish cleaning a home, a way of celebrating and finalising the process. If you are renting out your property it's the perfect way to clear the air before new guests arrive. If you would like to know more about this ancient practice just head over to my website and read more there. There's a link in the resources section.

14. VINEGAR

Vinegar is a multi-tasker and a go-to product for any cleaning jobs. Not only does it remove scale, it kills germs naturally and eliminates odours. A great way to descale kettles, taps and toilets, and to clean dirty tea and coffee cups.

Yes, it smells a little, but nothing like industrial products. Just add it to a spray bottle. When diluted it cleans windows perfectly.

Vinegar is also a superb alternative to washing powder. Mix it with salt (1/2 cup of white vinegar and 2 tablespoons of salt) or as a fabric softener in its own right. It doesn't leave your clothes smelling of vinegar as you might expect; they just smell fresh and clean. Vinegar also cleans out your washing machine, reduces scale, and takes out the soap residue clinging to pipes. Two jobs in one can't be bad!

15. VODKA

No, not for sneaky drinking while working, as mentioned in the quote at the beginning of this section! Vodka is a wonderful natural cleaner, producing a reflective shine on any metal or mirrored surface. Have a small bottle in your cleaning box for those stubborn stains.

My Top Ten Cleaning Hacks For Specific Areas

1. BATHS AND SHOWERS
One way to deal with these areas is to keep them as clean and dry as possible. If you leave a T-bar window cleaner and 'train' users to wipe away the excess water after their shower or bath, cleaning will be easier.

To unblock showerheads, remove them and place them in vinegar until the scale has dissloved.

Baking soda and vinegar will clean tiles and grout with just a small amount of effort.

2. COFFEE STAINS
Vinegar or baking soda and a little hot water will do the trick, just be patient.

3. FLOORS
Place 1/2 cup baking soda in a bucket of warm water, then all you have to do is mop.

4. FRIDGES
Clean with a 50/50 solution of vinegar and water, wipe clean and notice just how fresh the fridge now smells!

5. MIRRORS AND WINDOWS
Water and a microfibre cloth work well. You can also use neat vodka or white vinegar diluted in water. For really stubborn stains you may need to clean with Castile soap first, rinse off and then use the above.

6. OVENS
To clean an oven naturally you need a prodcut you won find in any shops - elbow grease! Don't let this put you of though; think of it as a muscle-building challenge, knowing that if you follow the instructions below, mother nature d most of the work for you overnight!

Spread a baking soda and water paste onto the insides your oven and leave overnight. The amount of paste yc need depends on how dirty your oven is. To begin, mix half a cup of baking soda with 3 tablespoons of water. An old paint brush is a fab way to get this over all the surfaces and shelves (avoid placing on the elements).

The next morning, use a damp cloth to wipe out as much of the paste and residue as you can. To remove the really dried-on areas you can spray with vinegar. Keep cleaning and using vinegar until your oven is shiny and clean again.

7. SINKS
Clean with bicarbonate of soda and vinegar by sprinkling the powder where it's needed in the sink and pouring a small amount of vinegar on top. As it foams rub gently into the dirty areas.

8. TAPS
Make a paste of vinegar and salt (1 teapsoon of vinegar and 1 tablespoon of salt) and use an old toothbrush to apply it to the scale. You can leave it there while you do the rest of the bathroom, then wipe it off and buff with a cloth

9. TOILET SCALE
Put a cup of vinegar in the toilet basin before you go to bed, and leave it overnight. Scrub well with the toilet brush and flush away the scale. Baking soda is also good for getting rid of stains. You can also add essential oils as you clean. Tea tree, lavender, and orange and lemon have antibacterial properties.
For really hard stains mix 1/2 cup of borax and 1/2 cup of vinegar.

10. WALLS
Fingerprints, pen marks and crayons can all be removed with baking soda and a cloth.

Rome Wasn't Built In A Day

Cleaning is neither difficult nor time-consuming. You have reached the end of this book and now understand the simple step-by-step process of cleaning. You know what modern supermarket cleaning products contain, and why it may be a good idea to avoid them. You also know how to make your own natural alternatives and how to use them around the home.

All that's left is for you to get your box or basket of goodies ready and get cleaning!
Thank you for reading all the way to the end. Even reading can be a huge task in a busy schedule when there's so much to be cleaned! Just remember that Rome wasn't built in a day. Take it slowly, remember the techniques I suggest, and I'm sure you'll do a great job.

I hope you've enjoyed this book and find the tips useful. Now I have shared my cleaning secrets, I look forward to hearing how you get on. If you have any other fabulous tips and tricks or cleaning hacks you would like to share you can find me through any of the links below.

I would love you to write a review so that others can decide whether this book is for them.

And Finally

While you were reading the book, I promised you two FREE gifts:

• Detox From Poisons In Personal Products
• Natural Toiletries For Stress Relief - Recipe Book

The usual format for getting these free gifts is to sign up to an automated mailing list where I can then bombard you with more 'stuff' whenever I decide to, which creates stress for both you and me. Stress for you, because your email box will contain more than ever, and stress for me because you probably won't even bother to open them!

Therefore, I would rather do things the old-fashioned and personal way. Send an email to me: kay(at)kay-newton.com. Put 'Cleaning Gifts' in the subject line and I will send you the two FREE gifts in pdf format directly to your inbox. This will be a personal message, typed by my own fingers, so please be patient! You may not receive an answer straight away, and you may have to remind me again if I haven't answered within a week!

Kx

PS. I promise not to share your contact details with any third parties.
PPS. If you want to write back, that's up to you. I will not open up any further conversations with you, unless that is what you would like to do.
PPPS. Now that you have cleaned your home it's time to focus on *you*! Head over to my website where you can download *The Art of Midlife Stress Busting - Seven Steps to Declutter Your Mind Without Pills or Potions* for FREE!

Resources

Please note, I am not affiliated to any of the companies below, and do not receive any financial commissions from them.

Stores to buy alternative natural products:
http://www.ethicalsuperstore.com/
http://www.bonami.com/index.php/products/powder_cleanser/
http://biokleenhome.com/shop-online/

Microfibre Cleaning System:
www.enjo.com/

Article about Plastic Pollution of the Oceans:
https://www.theguardian.com/environment/2016/jun/20/microfibers-plastic-pollution-oceans-patagonia-synthetic-clothes-microbeads

A possible solution to saving the ocean from microfibres:
https://www.kickstarter.com/projects/879498424/cora-ball-microfiber-catching-laundry-ball

Smudging Benefits -
https://www.kay-newton.com/smudge/

Bust Stress With Essential Oils -
https://www.kay-newton.com/essential-oils/

Borax -
https://wellnessmama.com/26407/borax-safe/

To Find Kay

Website: https://Kay-Newton.com
Facebook Page:
https://www.facebook.com/TheMidlifeStressBuster/
Facebook Group:
https://www.facebook.com/groups/MidlifeStressBusting

Other Books by Kay

Available through https://www.kay-newton.com/books/

The Art Of Midlife Stress Busting - Seven Steps To Declutter Your Mind Without Pills Or Potions
https://www.amazon.com/Art-Midlife-Stress-Busting-Declutter-ebook/dp/B072862TVN

Tips And Tricks For Stress-Free Downsizing - A Step by Step to Moving On
https://www.amazon.com/Tips-Tricks-Stress-Free-Downsizing-Moving-ebook/dp/B0722THJ3Z

To buy titles in the *Quick Fix* Series by Pat Duckworth and Kay Newton:

Quick Fix For Empty Nest Syndrome -
http://amzn.to/2pNRI8x

Quick Fix For Parents Living With Boomerang Kids -
http://amzn.to/2pgxuM2

Quick Fix For Giving Glorious Gifts -
http://amzn.to/2pd570A

Quick Fix For Your Meaningful Midlife Relationship -
http://amzn.to/2pNqVSc

Quick Fix For Decluttering - http://amzn.to/2qzD8NI

Quick Fix For Better Sleep - http://amzn.to/2qHCA5a

.

Printed in Great Britain
by Amazon